# Beautiful America's
# Atlanta

*Front Cover: Lake Clara Meer in Piedmont Park*

Published by
**Beautiful America Publishing Co.**
9725 S.W. Commerce Circle
Wilsonville, Oregon 97070


Design: Heather Kier
Editor: Andrea Tronslin
Linotronic Output: Digitype


**Library of Congress Catalog Number 96-672**
ISBN 0-89802-667-9
ISBN 0-89802-666-0 (Paperback)

*The State Capital Building*

# Beautiful America's

# Atlanta

Text and Photography
by Dennis Eugene Engleman

Beautiful America Publishing Company

# Contents

# Dedication

To Nicholas, Lily and Victoria,
whose joyful presence makes
their hometown Atlanta
the best place
on earth.

*Atlanta's pristine skyline*

*(Opposite) Dazzling downtown Atlanta*

Coastal States
EQUITABLE

# NEWFANGLED OLD-FASHIONED ATLANTA

Atlanta grapples ceaselessly with two extremes: "what was" and "what will be." The permanence of the past, the possibilities of the future . . . these opposing forces tend to push the present into puniness. Past and future galvanize attitudes and activity in this city like powerful magnets; mere "now" often seems no more than a postscript of the one or a prefiguration of the other.

Elsewhere, the future may emerge by measures from the past; in Atlanta it erupts like molten metal from a blast furnace. The city does not merely grow or progress in some mild-mannered way; it *ignites* into newness. Transforming—seemingly at will—before the astonished gaze of its inhabitants, Atlanta challenges the world to change with it.

Native Atlantan and world-famous novelist Pat Conroy describes his hometown as "the only city I know that has dedicated itself to the worship of newness."[1] Given Atlanta's symbol—the phoenix—such a view is understandable. Like this mythical bird which dies and rises again from its own ashes, Atlanta has been reborn time after time. It is a megalopolis in constant flux, forever transmuting itself into something more grandiose than before.

Henry Grady, the much-admired former editor of the *Atlanta Constitution*, declared in 1886 that the "*new* South is enamoured of her new work. Her soul is stirred with the breath of a new life." As leading representative of this New South, Atlanta has fully embodied that craze for newness which Grady articulated more than a century ago. To be at the forefront of the action, ahead of the times, up-to-the-minute, and hot off the press—all this is conveyed in the city's modish nickname, "Hotlanta."

And yet, "Hotlanta's" newness derives at least in part from juxtaposition—for the city is also firmly attached to the old. The struggles and sacrifices of her pioneers are honored, while her incomparable heritage is treasured more keenly with each passing year.

Ultimately, "what will be" and "what was" are each welcome here. While the future contends with the past for the present, "Atlanta-of-the-Ages" binds and blends them both. It stretches like a kudzu vine between antecedents and potentialities, maintaining roots in the Deep South while branching into the furthest reaches of high tech.

The very intensity of this dichotomous environment tends to produce visionaries, leaders capable of viewing both the future in terms of the past, and the past in terms of the future. Like the Biblical householder who "brings forth out of his treasure things old and new" (Matthew 13:52), such people have produced riches for themselves and their society by embracing these natural limits. Atlanta's history is abundant with personalities whose diligence, patience, and imagination have overcome seemingly insuperable obstacles. Their memorials can be seen in the schools, the churches, the art institutions, the spires of corporate headquarters—all peering respectfully over ancient Indian meeting grounds and Civil War battlefields.

Because of these leaders, Atlanta's importance passes beyond the merely regional. The city has dramatically impacted not only the South, but the United States, and not only the United States, but the world. For example, it was here that Coca-Cola was invented and climbed to world-wide soft drink dominance. It was here that Joel Chandler Harris wrote his Uncle Remus plantation stories, such as the memorable "Br'er Rabbit and the Tar Baby." It was here that Margaret Mitchell labored over *Gone With the Wind* while working as a reporter for the *Atlanta Journal* newspaper. It was here that Martin Luther King Jr. was born, preached at Ebenezer Baptist Church, and was laid to rest after his assassination. It was here that Ted Turner's Cable News Network got its start and continues to break ground in presenting information globally. It was here that Billy Payne's persistent efforts brought the 1996 Olympics to Georgia.

Atlanta has a singular success story which is a testament to its hard workers, of whom there are far too many to list. For all the city's magnificent buildings and superlative systems, Atlanta is really about . . . people. It is about folks from many backgrounds and various perspectives who have a common goal: to realize their hopes and dreams in this truly unique place.

# A PEACH OF A TOWN

In 1782 the chief of the Talassee Indians informed Georgia Governor John Martin that a war party of Coweta Indians had gathered near the Chattahoochee River at "the Standing Peachtree." What the Coweta tribe did that day is forgotten, but the fruit tree where they met has gone down in history. That tree apparently survived at least until the War of 1812, since a defensive bulwark built near it was named Fort Peachtree.

Travelers named the winding thirty-mile Indian trail between Fort Peachtree and Fort Daniel (north in Gwinnett County) Peachtree Road. As the city grew up around this conduit, a strange nostalgia for the patriarchal fruit afflicted those with the task of naming new streets—or perhaps they were short on imagination. In any case, over 55 streets now contain the word "Peachtree"—a

*Monoliths of Modernity*

*The Georgia-Pacific Building*

*Atlanta at dusk*

source of amusement, if not confusion, to visitors.

But even this excess of peachness was not enough for Georgians. Orchards were enthusiastically cultivated, and by 1930 there were 16 million peach trees in the state. The luscious fruit gained a national audience when Georgian Samuel H. Rumph invented a refrigerated wooden shipping crate. The peach gained official sanction when adopted in 1940 as the permanent symbol on state license plates.

Atlanta's annals are so linked to that peach of all streets—Peachtree Road—that a pilgrimage along this twisting thoroughfare is *de rigueur* for visitors. Such a journey does more than entertain; it presents a virtual historical narrative. The Peachtree Route begins downtown near the immense skeletal peach presiding over Interstate I-75/85. From there it wends north through midtown past another great skeletal peach, then to Buckhead and beyond, offering bountiful sights and insights into this most interesting of Southern cities.

# THE PEACHTREE
# ROUTE: DOWNTOWN

In 1833 the Georgia legislature chartered three new railroad lines: The Central Railroad and Canal Company, to run to the coast at Savannah; the Georgia Railroad Company, to run west from Augusta; and the Monroe Railroad, to run north from Macon. It also established a point at which these lines would meet, called the "Zero Mile Post." The selection was based strictly on favorable topography, with minimal expectations as to the site's commercial future. In fact, Stephen Long, chief engineer for the Western and Atlantic Railroad, declared the area "would be a good location for one tavern, a blacksmith shop, a grocery store and nothing else!" Future Mayor James Calhoun added, "The terminus of that railroad will never be more than an eating house."

These predictions were destined not to come true, perhaps because the speakers did not grasp the trinitarian power of a *synaxis*—or meeting—of three ways (in this case, railroads). Though the town's pragmatic origins were evident in its nickname, "Terminus," grander things lay in store.

In 1845, Terminus was officially renamed Atlanta, a word whose mythic connotations suggested some extraordinary destiny. The new name promoted a correspondingly new sense of identity— whereas Terminus represented an ending point, Atlanta would henceforth signify new beginnings. Jonathan Norcross, whose boldness would have been impertinent had it not been prophetic, immediately petitioned the state to make Atlanta Georgia's capital.

As though eager to fulfill its novel fate, the city suddenly surged with growth. The "tavern, blacksmith shop, and grocery store" gave way to more far-reaching enterprises. Five Points, where the railroads met, erupted with warehouses, machine shops, hotels and stores.

Atlanta proved to be an opportunist's treasure trove. Prospects of prosperity attracted hordes, and the population exploded from 2,500 in 1847 to 7,500 ten years later. Newspapers, schools, banks and hospitals sprang up in this new center of southern industry and commerce. By 1864 the population had reached 23,000 and the city was so strategic to the South's cause in the Civil War that General William Tecumseh Sherman specifically targeted it for his version of "urban renewal." As Diane Coulter Thomas noted, "Richmond may have been the Confederacy's political heart, but Atlanta was its nerve center, its transportation hub, supply base, and munitions depot."[2]

# A Citadel Under Siege

The Battle of Atlanta was decisive for the South, which depended heavily on the city's rail lines and manufacturing strength. Aware that Atlanta held the key to the Confederacy's ability to perpetuate the Civil War, General Sherman determined to invade.

Approaching from the North, Sherman was stopped by Confederate General Joseph E. Johnston's troops for two weeks at Kennesaw Mountain. Sherman occupied Big Shanty, but was unable to dislodge Johnston from his superior position. After sustaining three thousand casualties, the Union general adopted a flanking strategy which drove the battle front steadily closer to Atlanta.

In desperation, Confederate President Jefferson Davis replaced cautious Johnston with General John B. Hood. Though Hood's boldness had already cost him an arm and leg, he recklessly threw Rebel troops against the Federals on July 22, 1864, initiating the Battle of Atlanta. Gaining no victory while losing thousands of irreplaceable soldiers, Hood retreated to the circle of forts on the city's perimeter and challenged Sherman not to shell them. Sherman charged Hood with cowardice for "hiding" among noncombatants, and reminded him that war was, after all, "the science of barbarism."

After enduring a four-week siege, Hood evacuated his troops and left residents to fend for themselves. Atlanta officially fell September 2, when Mayor James M. Calhoun surrendered with a hand-penciled note. The victorious Sherman paused in the city until November 14, then meted out an unparalleled punishment: except for a handful of buildings, such as City Hall, the Church of the Immaculate Conception, and the Masonic Lodge, Atlanta was incinerated.

Atlanta thus became the first and only major American city to be destroyed in war—a blow from which she was not intended to recover. Satisfied with his handiwork, Sherman then set off on the

*The Georgia "Peach" looms over downtown*

*(Opposite) Dogwood delight*

infamous but effective March to the Sea, burning a hundred-mile-wide swath through the South.

The Battle of Atlanta is vividly illustrated in a unique setting called the Cyclorama. Located in historic Grant Park, this cylindrical building contains an immense diorama. A forty-two foot-high, nine thousand pound, circular painting was created by a team of artists in 1865, when the details of the battle and of old Atlanta were still fresh in memory.

The Cyclorama depicts this conflict from a 360-degree perspective, as though an observer stood in the very center of the action. Railroad tracks, shrapnelled trees, cannons, and other three-dimensional elements blend with the painted surface as viewers watch from a slowly rotating platform.

In the Cyclorama lobby is the locomotive *Texas,* which dueled with another steam engine, the *General,* in 1862. The *General,* on display at the Big Shanty Museum in Kennesaw, was bound from Atlanta to Chattanooga one April morning. While its crew ate breakfast at the small town of Big Shanty, this 2-2-0 locomotive of the Western & Atlantic Railroad was stolen by Union sympathizers. "Andrew's Raiders," as they were called, led a high speed race north until the *General's* brass journals overheated and began to melt. Confederate pursuers in the Texas eventually captured the Federal raiders, and most of them were hanged in downtown Atlanta. William Pittenger escaped, made it to Union lines, and later wrote *The Great Locomotive Chase.*

# Resurrection!

Grabbing hold of its bootstraps, the city-that-refused-to-die hauled itself up from the dust of destruction. Literally rising from the ashes, Atlanta reincarnated itself from the "pre-fired" bricks which were all that remained of most buildings. In spite of devastation and the war's aftermath, Atlantans pressed on, determined to survive. Witnessing this amazing resurrection, this *Resurgens* (now the city's official motto), the *New York Herald* exulted, "these Americans have gathered together the wreckage and out of it have built a structure which is stupendous in its majesty and its promise of the future."

Having survived being a wartime "hot spot," the city soon surpassed its previous importance as an economic, political, and cultural hot spot. Rebuilt railroads created the vortex of an industrial/commercial whirlpool whose currents rippled through the entire South. Atlanta soon became the logical choice for Georgia's governmental centers, and by 1885 (just fifty years after engineer Long's inauspicious report), a cornerstone was laid near the Zero Mile Post for a new State Capital Building.

The capital dome was topped by an unusual present, given by the state of Ohio in 1884.

*Plotting a "Sherman's Flank"*

*Dreams of "Br' er Rabbit"*

Supposedly a gesture of reconciliation, the gift was a statue of a woman bearing a sword and lighted torch. Although she is said to represent Freedom, a more apt title might be Phoenix Flambé, as the figure's weapons vividly call to mind Sherman's devastation.

Georgia has experienced more than one kind of burning; in 1828 gold was discovered in the North Georgia mountains. Thousands of men came down with gold fever during this period. When their inflammation finally cooled off, some were very wealthy while others were as poor as before.

To help memorialize the "yellow fever" conflagration, a wagon train full of genuine twenty three-karat gold endured an eighty-mile ride from Dahlonega's mountains to Atlanta in 1958. The capital's dome was sheathed with a gleaming forty-three ounces of this native metal, which now shimmers like a jeweled crown in the southern sky.

# Building a Heritage

The railroad was Atlanta's original *raison d'être,* and has continued to be vitally important. As the city grew, trains hauling raw materials north and manufactured goods south chugged through at an ever-increasing rate. Growth in commerce came at the price of congestion, however. By the late 1800s, crossing ten sets of railroad tracks at Forsyth Street had become a risky proposition, especially for slow-moving wagons and pedestrians.

This danger was averted when in 1891 viaducts began to be built over the railroad tracks. The benefit had a commercial aspect in keeping with Atlanta's entrepreneurial spirit—it made the downtown more accessible to a new invention: the automobile. These viaducts created a raised street level over a six-block area. Not only did this give the shopping area an entirely different look, but also it created a need for new store entrances on what had formerly been second floors.

The buildings below the viaducts were subsequently abandoned, which ironically preserved their historic character. In the 1980s this long-ignored area was reopened and fittingly named Underground Atlanta. The original streets and storefronts have been refurbished, offering visitors a unique look at the earliest days of the city. With the addition of over 150 new shops, restaurants, and ongoing top-notch entertainment, Underground Atlanta has become an ultra-popular gathering spot.

Atlanta Heritage Row, also located in Underground Atlanta, documents the city's turbulent past and its rise to world prominence. Beginning in 1840s Terminus, as the city was then known, visitors pass through six interactive historical exhibition, replete with sights and sounds. Within a Civil War bomb shelter, one hears projectiles exploding. In the next phase, rebuilding from the war, Henry Grady's "New South" speech rings out in the context of John Philip Sousa's "King

Cotton March". Following this, blues music throbs aboard a 1920s trolley, while the career of Margaret Mitchell is reviewed. Stirring speeches of Dr. Martin Luther King, Jr. recall the Civil Rights era, while cryptic radio messages of air traffic controllers at Hartsfield International Airport bring visitors into the present.

# The City's Most Popular Invention

On May 8, 1886, druggist Dr. John Styth Pemberton concocted a tasty batch of syrup in his backyard on Marietta Street. He described his potion as an "Ideal Brain Tonic," but it was not until mixed with fizzy water at Jacob's Drugstore that its real pizzazz was unlocked. The beverage was named after two of its ingredients, the coca leaf and the kola nut. Two weeks later on May 29th, the first print ad for Coca-Cola appeared in the *Atlanta Journal.* The famous hourglass bottle was created in 1916 by Charles Rainwater, and later received the honor of being officially registered as a trademark.

During World War II, General Dwight Eisenhower requested machinery for operating Coke bottling plants (sixty-four were established) as close as possible to combat areas in order to keep up morale among American soldiers. Over the years Coke has become the world's favorite soft drink, being asked for more than 300 million times a day in eighty languages around the globe. The *World of Coca-Cola,* located next to Underground Atlanta, is an interactive museum dedicated to this tastiest of Southern concoctions.

# THE PEACHTREE ROUTE: MIDTOWN

Several miles north of downtown's commercial and governmental maelstrom, the area called Midtown has emerged as a distinct focal point of business and culture. In a high-energy synthesis of styles, the Occidental Grand Hotel, Promenade Two, One Atlantic Center, Club Suites, Colony Square, the Campanile, Wyndham Hotel, and other new buildings rub shoulders with each other, offering a stunning variety of modern work and living spaces. These gargantuan structures metamorphose from daytime understatement to nighttime hyperbole under the influence of spectacular lighting.

Southern soldiers

(Opposite) Realistic Civil War engagements

Midtown is also a lively locus of local arts, the home base of at least two dozen artistic organizations. The High Museum of Art and the Woodruff Arts Center are the most prominent, presenting world-class theatric, symphonic, and visual art experiences.

The "Fabulous" Fox Theatre has gripped the imagination of Atlantans since it opened on Christmas Day, 1929. That first program, costing fifteen cents, included dancing girls, a community sing, music on the 3,610-pipe Moller organ, an orchestral interlude conducted by Enrico Leide, the first Mickey Mouse cartoon, and a feature film called *Salute*.

The theatre was part of a Masonic lodge, whose elaborate motifs conveyed the mystique of a tented Moorish mosque. Patrons settling into their seats were enveloped in a desert courtyard ambience. As the orange glow of sunset faded, twinkling stars fitfully appeared and soft clouds drifted across an azure sky. Entertainers of the silver screen thus frequently found their medium itself a hard act to follow. The Fox retains its position even today as a premier setting for opera, ballet, Broadway plays, and wide-screen, stereophonic films.

In 1926, Margaret Mitchell, a sixth-generation Atlantan, began work on her only novel, *Gone With the Wind.* Much of the writing was done in a dilapidated Midtown apartment building which Mitchell irreverently dubbed "the dump." Perhaps the archaic setting provided creative inspiration. In 1936 her book became a best-seller and later an Academy Award-winning movie starring Clark Gable and Vivien Leigh. Margaret Mitchell's depiction of the Battle of Atlanta, and of the destitute condition of the city in the aftermath of the flames, has immortalized this searing episode in American history.

For many years, *Gone With the Wind* outsold every book except the Bible. Its popularity has served to communicate a story more poignant than mere romance, and to show that the South lost not just a war in the 1800s, but a culture and a way of life.

Piedmont Park is central Atlanta's most popular open recreational area. The Midtown location makes the park easily accessible; strollers, skaters, and loungers enjoy its open prospects all year round. The park grounds have been a farm, a Civil War encampment, a driving club, and much more. It was here that the 1885 Cotton States and International Exposition drew the world's attention with Booker T. Washington's memorable speech on race relations (called the "Atlanta Compromise"), John Philip Sousa's presentation of the "King Cotton March," and the nation's first public showing of movies. Yet, Piedmont Park's most spectacular enterprise was probably the 1887 Piedmont Exposition, attended by President Grover Cleveland and even the city's former anathema, William T. Sherman. These days, Piedmont Park serves as the finish line of the Peachtree Road

Race and annually hosts many events, such as the Dogwood Festival and the Atlanta Arts Festival.

Midtown's Woodruff Arts Center is home base for the Atlanta Symphony Orchestra. In 1995 the orchestra celebrated its fiftieth year with a national TV broadcast of "Gospel Christmas," a concerto recording with Andre Watts, and a critically praised Carnegie Hall concert. Under the baton of Romanian-born Israeli conductor Yoel Levi, this orchestra has gained international distinction. Yet it traditionally maintains hometown ties with a series of free outdoor summer concerts in Piedmont Park, Grant Park, or Chastain Park, which draw casual crowds fond of the lawnchair ambience of candles and wine.

The appliance-white exterior of the High Museum of Art suggests the embodiment of modernity. Winding, scenic ramps and galleries punctuated by views into neighboring galleries create the effect of a museum which is integral to the displayed art. Richard Meier's novel design won the American Institute of Architects Honor Award as one of the top ten buildings of the 1980s. The High Museum houses over 7,000 objects, including contemporary art, an unequalled collection of nineteenth- and twentieth-century American furniture, European paintings and sculpture, African masks, folk art and photography.

The Rhodes House is a grand testimonial for a rags-to-riches entrepreneur. Although Amos Rhodes came to Atlanta in 1875 with only seventy-five dollars in his pocket, he started a chain of furniture stores which still dominate the local market. In 1904 Rhodes built a stone mansion in the Victorian Romanesque Revival style, which was modeled after Rhineland castles in Germany. The stunning interior boasts a carved mahogany staircase and a series of stained glass windows depicting "The Rise and Fall of the Confederacy."

# THE PEACHTREE
# ROUTE: BUCKHEAD

Buckhead owes its rustic name to Henry Irby's marksmanship. In 1838, Irby operated a tavern and grocery store near Peachtree Road. One day Irby shot a deer nearby and mounted the buck's head on a post. Visitors apparently decided that Buckhead was a more inviting and appropriate moniker than Irbyville, and the name stuck.

Irby's entrepreneurial spirit as well as his name lives on, and the area has become a beehive of sophisticated financial and social pacesetting. Buckhead is one of the wealthiest neighborhoods in

*Confederate graves are remembered*

*The Cyclorama*

*Cyclorama and diorama, where two dimensions become three*

the United States, with more than 100 homes valued over one million dollars. Shops in Lenox Square Mall and Phipps Plaza vie for offering the trendiest accoutrements, while Hotel Nikko, Swissôtel, and the Ritz-Carlton Buckhead provide elegant accommodations.

The Atlanta History Center began humbly in a converted residence on Peachtree Street. When Louise Allen, one of the founding members, learned that the Swan House was for sale, she convinced the board that it should be purchased. The acquisition of this centerpiece of Atlanta's legacy established the course of preservation which the center still follows. It now maintains one of the largest museums of urban and suburban history in the United States.

Located on the grounds of the Atlanta History Center, the Tullie Smith Farm was built in the 1840s. The farm buildings may appear primitive and plain, but they are actually more typical of Georgia's plantation period than the large mansions romantically associated with the Deep South. Upland settlers who built such accommodations were typically of Scotch, Irish or English descent, and knew how to be self-sufficient. The house, kitchen, barn, corncrib, dairy, smokehouse, and cabin belonged to many generations of the Smith family, the last member of which was Tullie Smith, who died in 1967.

The event by which Peachtree Road best known these days is the annual Peachtree Road Race. This run weaves from Buckhead's Lenox Square Mall south to placid Piedmont Park every Fourth of July, drawing world-class athletes from as far away as Poland and Australia. Of over three thousand 10-kilometer road races in the nation, the Peachtree is by far the largest. In 1995, an amazing fifty thousand runners participated, while thousands more cheered from sidewalks all along the 6.2-mile course. 60 percent of the participants were Atlantans ranging in age from ten to eighty-three.

Named for Georgia's founder James Edward Oglethorpe, *Oglethorpe University* was established in the early 1800s to train Presbyterian ministers. It is said that the old university died at Gettysburg, for "during the Civil War its students were soldiers, its endowment was lost in confederate bonds, and its buildings were used for barracks and hospitals."[3] Like most other Atlanta institutions, the university suffered Sherman's scathing touch.

After the war, Thormwell Jacobs decided to rebuild the devastated university to look like an English countryside school. The major buildings of Oglethorpe were designed in the Gothic Revival style of Oxford's Corpus Christi College. The resulting British atmosphere is an ideal setting for such annual events as the Atlanta Celtic Festival and the Georgia Shakespeare Festival.

Jacobs was an innovator, and one of his noteworthy contributions was the Oglethorpe Crypt of

Civilization. This is the world's largest and most extensive time capsule, buried beneath Phoebe Hall in 1940. It contains a detailed record of human achievement from ancient times to the middle of the twentieth century, and is not to be opened until 8113.

# A CITY ON A HILL

"A city that is set on a hill cannot be hid," declares Matthew's Gospel. Nestled in the foothills of the Blue Ridge Mountains, Atlanta is definitely visible. At an elevation of 1,050 feet, it is the second highest major city in the United States. The air at this altitude produces brilliant, almost lunar-stark, images of city life.

Below the skyscrapers, twelve lanes of Interstate 75/85 snake around downtown like a cobra trapped in a basket. The lifeblood of industry courses these serpentine arteries daily, pulsating to the rhythms of rush hour. The "newer" the city becomes, the more it does seem to rush, and Federal highway officials have reported that "Atlanta's traffic is the fastest of any major city in the nation."[4] Yet above this cacophonous cadence of commercialism, with its modules of mass mobilization, Atlanta-of-the-Ages serenely watches.

International Boulevard juts off I-75/85, then curves graciously toward a melange of international color. This is downtown's VIP entrance—the main thoroughfare between the hotel district and the vast offerings of central Atlanta. Wide sidewalks, globally-recognized symbols, and a an expanse of flags reassure the visitor that he has entered a foreign-friendly environment. Signs offer directions to the Georgia Dome, World Congress Center, Underground Atlanta, and other popular spots. World-class accommodations beckon, including the Marriott Marquis, largest convention hotel south of New York, the Westin Peachtree Plaza, tallest in the country, and the Hilton, resembling an enormous washing-machine agitator.

Atlanta's international face is becoming increasingly pronounced among a population which is only 60 percent native. Immigrants have always played a vital role in the city's history, but now they are doing more to preserve and promote their own cultural and religious roots. International festivals occur regularly, as German, Russian, Irish, Greek, Mexican, Chinese, Japanese, and other national groups celebrate. The Hibernian Benevolent Society of Atlanta sponsors an annual Saint Patrick's Day parade which is one of the nation's oldest. Many foreign-language publications and TV shows are produced here, and over one thousand foreign-owned companies have established

The railroad and MARTA

(Opposite) The locomotive "General"

operations in the city.

Atlanta is a city on a hill in many respects. With a world-class international airport, three converging interstate highways (another important *synaxis* of three ways), and the proximity of Georgia's deepwater ports, it is a major transportation hub. Named by *Fortune* in 1991 as "America's Best City for Business," and with offices of over 730 Fortune 1,000 companies, Atlanta is a major commercial hub. As headquarters for CNN, Headline News, TNT, and TBS Superstation, thirty-eight radio stations, eight television stations and nine daily newspapers, it is also a major communications hub.

To top all this off, Atlanta is also one of the nation's busiest convention sites, serving this industry in style with the Georgia World Congress Center. The vast complex regularly hosts Southpack, Comdex, the Super Show, the Atlanta Home Furnishings Market, the Yager Free Enterprise Show, the International Gift Market, the National Model Railroaders Association, the Bobbin Show and more. It manages multiple events with ease, providing both vendors and attendees with extraordinary levels of service.

# TRADITIONS OF GRACIOUS LIVING

In the spring, Atlanta is awash in dogwood and azalea blossoms. Summer is announced by the pearl-white delight of magnolia, that venerable matriarch of Southern flowers. Through the warm months and into fall, pink and magenta sprays of crepe myrtle dance in the shimmering sky.

Even with its temperate climate, Atlanta feels the change of four seasons. Snow, however, is a rare (though welcome!) visitor. Flowers often bloom outdoors year round, lending a colorful palette to the city's historic dwellings.

Many of the nation's most significant personalities have crafted careers in Atlanta, fashioning their homes to reflect their distinctive tastes.

After he found a family of birds in his mailbox, Joel Chandler Harris christened his home the Wren's Nest. This prosaic name hints at Harris' preoccupation with the folksy side of life on the "West End," Atlanta's oldest neighborhood (circa 1835). He was a writer for the *Atlanta Constitution*, but is best known for preserving plantation stories of the old South.

Harris loved to write while sitting in a high-backed rocking chair on his front porch. From there he scrutinized passers-by while reflecting on the slave narratives he had heard as a child. Harris immortalized these stories in books such as *The Tales of Uncle Remus*. His "Br'er Rabbit and the Tar Baby" is perhaps the best known of these, having been animated by Walt Disney in "Song of the South."

Born into slavery in 1858, Alonzo Herndon became America's first black millionaire. He began his ascent to wealth by opening the Crystal Palace Barbershop on Peachtree Street, in which he could not have gotten his own hair cut. The success of this enterprise led him to found the Atlanta Life Insurance Company, now the largest black-owned insurance company in America. His beautiful beaux arts-style Herndon Home was built by black craftsmen in 1910. The fifteen-room, columned mansion is still furnished with rare Venetian and Roman glass dating to 200 B.C., and stands as a testament to Herndon's enterprise and resolve.

The Swan House, which derives its nickname from the swan motifs throughout, was designed in the Anglo-Palladian style by Philip Trammel Shutze. Shutze adapted classical symmetry to the twentieth century, creating what some consider his most memorable and successful work. The home was built in the 1920s for Edward Inman, a wealthy businessman whose fortune stemmed largely from cotton.

Emily Inman lived in the Swan House until 1965, and the building remains essentially as she left it. Most of the furnishings are original. Hand-painted English wallpaper, hand-carved woodwork, and seventeenth century antiques combine with modern "simplicity," as evidenced in the flowing, free-standing stairway. The house and its twenty-six-acre tract were purchased by the Atlanta History Center and are now available for public tours.

Grant Park began as a Confederate Army encampment (Fort Walker) overlooking downtown, which Colonel Lemuel P. Grant built on his own land. After the Civil War, Colonel Grant donated the property to the city for a park and it became one of the premier holiday sites of the South. Boating and swimming at the park's Lake Abana were prime attractions, while picnics and a zoo full of exotic animals also drew crowds to the Parisian-like setting.

An immense four hundred-foot circular painting of the Battle of Atlanta—the Cyclorama—was put on permanent display in Grant Park, and beautiful Victorian homes eventually spread around it as far as Oakland Cemetery. While the luxurious lake is now gone, many community events still take place in this forested setting, including the Atlanta Jazz Festival and free performances by the Atlanta Symphony Orchestra.

In 1924 President Franklin D. Roosevelt began to treat his polio in the curative waters of Warm

*Reminiscing*

*Fishing in the "New South"*



*(Opposite) Piedmont Park*

*Georgia freight depot, downtown's oldest building*

*Underground Atlanta*

*World of Coca-Cola offers a total soft drink experience*

*Coca-Cola Corporate Headquarters*

*The Fox Theatre's oriental opulance*

*The fabulous Fox*

*Inside The Fox Theatre*

*The High Museum of Art*

*The Phodes House—A bit of Germany in Georgia*

*The Buckhead Financial District*

*Buckhead's glitzy appeal*

Phipps Plaza

*The beautiful interior of Phipps Plaza*

*Atlanta History Center*

*Tullie Smith Farm*

*The Peach Tree Road Race*

Springs. This village south of Atlanta was the American Lourdes; the president returned forty times, sampling banjo picking and moonshine along the way. As Roosevelt grew to understand the problems of rural Georgians, they in turn befriended him. The Roosevelt is a witness to this civic esteem. The blue-domed building named after the former president served for many years as a public high school, but has since been converted to quality in-town apartments.

The Robert Burns House, just east of Grant Park, was never occupied by Robert Burns. It is instead an exact copy of the cottage in Scotland in which the famous poet was born. Since being built in 1911, it has been used by the Robert Burns Club, which was formed in 1896 on the 137th anniversary of the death of its namesake. Celebrations called *ceilidh* preserve the Scottish traditions of piping, singing, and dancing.

Atlanta's first suburb, Inman Park, was created in the 1890s. Live oak trees transplanted from the coast a century ago continue to shade the neighborhood's lazy, inviting streets.

Many prominent Atlantans built their homes in Inman Park, including Asa Candler, founder of the Coca-Cola Company. The city's first electric trolley line travelled from downtown to the trolley barn that still presides over the annual Inman Park Spring Festival.

The heart of Inman Park is the quaint district known as Little Five Points. It has been popular for generations, and many of the city's early business leaders enjoyed strolling its curved sidewalks. Nowadays the area is something of a little Bohemia, flaunting the latest music, fashion, and mannerisms. Sidewalk coffee shops offer scenic exposure to itinerant musicians and poets.

# MELDING MINDS

Although as a frontier town Atlanta went seven years without a school, the city is now served by twenty-seven public educational systems operating 702 elementary through high school level institutions, and thirty-six degree-granting colleges. Local schools play a vital role in preparing Atlantans to meet the challenges of an increasingly complex world.

As early as 1927 Atlanta had the most imposing collection of historically black colleges and universities in the United States, a distinction which it maintains to this day. Started by former slaves as a grammar school, the Atlanta University System now consists of six institutions—Clark Atlanta University, The Interdenominational Theological Center, Morehouse School of Medicine, Spelman College, Morris Brown College, and Morehouse College—which set the standard for

Oglethorpe University

*International Boulevard*

African-American education throughout the country.

Morehouse is the nation's only historically black, all-male, four year liberal arts college; its alumni includes Nobel Peace Prize laureate Martin Luther King, Jr., Olympic gold medalist Edwin Moses, and award-winning filmmaker Spike Lee. Combined with the Interdenominational Theological Seminary and the Morehouse School of Medicine, the institutions of the Atlanta University comprise the world's largest black educational complex.

Agnes Scott College was the inspiration of ex-Confederate cavalry colonel and Savannah entrepreneur George C. Scott, and is named after his mother. This Presbyterian school began as the Decatur Female Seminary in 1889, and in 1907 became the first accredited college in Georgia.

The Georgia Institute of Technology is widely regarded as Atlanta's technological ace-in-the-hole. With a research budget bettered only by M.I.T. and Johns Hopkins, the school spews out nearly 2,000 highly trained engineers a year. Its thirty million dollar Manufacturing Research Center is unique in the country. This facility is dedicated to developing higher quality, lower cost manufacturing techniques. The school's Advanced Technologies Development Center focuses on creating new industries. The effect on the city is significant, as a majority of Atlanta's present high-tech companies began locally.

Emory University was established by Southern Methodists, and philanthropized by Coca-Cola. Asa Candler donated over a million dollars and seventy-five acres of land to move the campus to Atlanta, which accounts for its nickname, "Coke U." The school's dedication to education embraces, in the words of its namesake Bishop John Emory, "the whole wide scope of the character, condition, and interests of man, physical, mental, moral and religious, for time and eternity."

Emory University is enhanced by the presence of the Centers for Disease Control, the Center for International Studies, the Yerkes Primate Research Center, the Law Economics Center, and the National Humanities faculty. But the school's phenomenal success and broad influence are due, no doubt, to the underlying Christian code which its bylaws affirm: "maintaining unwavering devotion to the faith once for all delivered to the saints."

In addition to educational institutions, Atlanta has a rapidly growing home-schooling community. Home-schooled children, presently totalling around 1 percent of the student population across Georgia, are in good company: George Washington, Abraham Lincoln, Thomas Edison, Albert Einstein and Sandra Day O'Connor were all home-schooled at some point. Such students get the personalized attention which fosters scholastic excellence. New York City's Teacher of the Year John Taylor Gatto reports that "home-schooled students score significantly better than their conventionally-schooled peers on achievement tests."[5] As the *Atlanta Journal* noted appreciatively, "high test scores and good college admission records show it can work."[6]

# GLORY BE TO GOD!

In 1847 the first house of worship was erected on Peachtree Road, and Atlanta early on acquired the reputation of a "city of churches." Today over two thousand churches, representing forty religious denominations, provide Atlantans with abundant opportunity to worship God.

Peachtree Presbyterian Church is the largest of its denomination east of the Mississippi, while the Cathedral of St. Philip is the largest Episcopal church in the country. Ebenezer Baptist Church is famous as the site of Dr. Martin Luther King, Jr.'s early preaching. Dr. King was actually the third generation of King pastors to minister to this church over a period of seventy years.

Atlanta is also uniquely honored with the first church in the United States (and in the world) dedicated to St. John Maximovitch. This true modern day saint, who performed many documented miracles and died on American soil, was canonized in 1994 when his body was discovered to be incorrupt (undecayed) after more than twenty-five years. He is memorialized by the Saint John Maximovitch Eastern Orthodox Church, located in historic Grant Park.

# BREATHING SPACES

In Atlanta, people have both room to move and unique places to move to. The city is lush with conifers which give it the appearance of an urban forest. The brilliant green of pine contrasts with the striking red of Georgia clay, suggesting a perpetual Christmas scene. Atlanta also offers many neighborhood parks and lakes, and an efficient, accessible public transportation system (MARTA).

Much of Atlanta's urban landscape is ornamented by encroaching kudzu. This much-maligned plant was first displayed in the Japanese Pavilion at 1876's United States Centennial Exposition. At that time, Southerners loved its ability to provide ground cover at the rate of one hundred feet per year. Unfortunately, the plant could not be limited to designated areas. Kudzu spreads wildly, covering lawns and native trees, even railroad tracks. Its quivering tendrils climb through fences, over walls, and up guy wires to create a menagerie of vague, colossal shapes confounding identifi-

*World Congress Center*

*Trade Show at World Congress Center*

cation. On the positive side, it has great food value, both for humans and livestock. It is as good a fodder as alfalfa, the roots can be converted to tofu, and the vines woven into strong baskets.

Virginia-Highland began as a bungalow neighborhood, easily accessible to downtown by trolley. Virginia-Highland's proximity to Emory University has made it a popular hangout for artists and young professionals who want easygoing, in-town living. Relaxed sidewalk cafes and bookstores offer ongoing opportunities for kicking back.

Between 1850 and 1884, nearly every person who died in Atlanta was buried at Oakland Cemetery. At eighty-eight acres, it is the third largest green space in the city, following Piedmont and Grant Parks. The cemetery is the resting place of twenty-four former Atlanta mayors, Gone With the Wind author Margaret Mitchell, golfing champion Bobby Jones, and nearly three thousand Confederate soldiers. Seven of the Andrews Raiders were buried here until in 1887 when they were moved to Chattanooga. Oakland was part of the "rural cemetery movement," which viewed graveyards as city parks dedicated to contemplation of beauty and eternity. Classical, pagan, and Christian symbolism complete the pastoral setting.

Historic Marietta looks unchanged from when it was little more than a breakfast stop on the Atlanta-Chattanooga steam train run. The town's relaxed pace is a match for its classic Victorian architecture.

Marietta Square was based on a Savannah-like plan of gridded streets relieved by a central park. Glover Park is the heart of Marietta Square, while the square is in turn the heart of the community. Here countrified art festivals and evening outdoor concerts under the gazebo are routine. Bench-sitters enjoy the musically cascading waters of a grand fountain before heading over to the Kennesaw House, a Civil War-era hotel, for family-style Southern dinners.

Old Chamblee still retains its rustic atmosphere of country shops along a rail line. Although the area was gradually surrounded by modern development, it derived a new identity as on oasis for antique hunters.

# STUPENDOUS STONE MOUNTAIN

Northeast of downtown is a great granite knuckle from which emanates a timeless sense of mystique. Stone Mountain was a meeting place for Creek Indians for centuries before white settlers arrived, and blackened signal pits can still be seen on the mountain's top. In 1790, George

Washington sent his friend Colonel Marinus Willett there to try to settle differences between the warring Creeks and other tribes. In his *Narrative of Military Actions*, Willett records that "while I was at Stony Mountain, I ascended the summit. It is one solid rock of a circular form about one mile across."

Willett's report was conservative. The eight-hundred-foot-high mountain is actually the largest exposed mass of granite in the world, and its immense distinctive shape never fails to evoke awe. "In the glare of the midday sun the huge rock seems to move as it shimmers with the heat . . . During a storm the sides of the mountain become a mighty waterfall . . . After the storm its sides are streaked with rivulets of silver and it glows with a radiant freshness . . . Late in the afternoon its majesty is emphasized by a purple haze . . . When partly shrouded by mist or fog, the ancient stone appears to cling to the secrets of its mysterious past . . . About twice a century it is glorified by a rainbow which starts at its base, climbs the side and seems to leave a pot of gold on the summit . . ."[7]

Legend has it that the Indians eventually sold the mountain for "a musket and a jackass." The settlers who bought the rock considered it nearly worthless and in their turn reportedly traded it for "a muzzle-loading gun and $20." Today it is worth over thirty million dollars.

Not long after the Civil War, the United Daughters of the Confederacy conceived the idea of creating a giant memorial on the mountain's side. It was not until 1970 however, that the three-acre image was completed. This is the world's largest bas-relief sculpture carving, portraying Confederate President Jefferson Davis, General Robert E. Lee, and General Thomas "Stonewall" Jackson on horseback. The figures are so immense that elegant luncheons with full dining room staff have been carried out on Robert E. Lee's shoulder.

A Swiss skylift offers a stunning ascent and a bird's-eye view of the carvings. On top of Stone Mountain grow unique flora that are present nowhere else in the state. At its base are the original train tracks which were used in the 1800s for quarrying granite. The Stone Mountain railroad now follows this circuitous route, giving visitors a dazzling view of the entire mountain

The thirty-two hundred acre park offers many other pleasures, such as paddle wheel steamboat rides, nightly laser shows on the rock face, and a sizable collection of authentic antebellum buildings. Plantation homes and slave dwellings from the 1800s reveal that while daily existence required more manual effort, it was not necessarily lacking in refinement and comfort.

Festivals celebrate Georgia's colorful past throughout the year. Whittlers, broom-makers, weavers and blacksmiths preserve crafts that were common a century ago. Reenactments of the life and times of earlier days, even of specific Civil War battles with black-powder firearms and authentic uniforms, help modern Southerners recall their roots.

The Wren's Nest

(Opposite) The Herndon Home

Nestled at the foot of Stone Mountain is Stone Mountain village, where the police station and courthouse rub shoulders in the old brick railroad depot beneath overhanging clumps of mistletoe. This nineteenth century hamlet is something of a tourist's paradise—a picturesque gaggle of over ninety shops, galleries, and restaurants offering Southern crafts and local food specialties such as jambalaya, fried alligator, and pecan pie. At the annual Sugarplum Festival, old Saint Nicholas himself is said to appear.

# A SOUTHERN LOVE
# FOR THE ARTS

The laid-back legacy of Dixie fosters a fondness for what is classic and beautiful. Since its early days, Atlanta has promoted the arts. The first theatre was built in 1854, and during the 1860s Kimball's Opera House was a popular attraction. Performances by the Metropolitan Opera became an annual tradition, featuring such great performers as Geraldine Farrar and Enrico Caruso. Oscar Wilde lectured here, Rudolf Valentino courted silver screen viewers, Helen Keller drew crowds. Atlanta is home to the nation's oldest continuously playing ballet company and the critically acclaimed Atlanta Opera, as well as the Atlanta Virtuosi, the Atlanta Music Club, the Center for Puppetry Arts, and many others.

Midtown's Woodruff Arts Center is unique in the U.S. for combining the visual and performing arts. The center consists of the High Museum of Art, the Metropolitan Memorial Arts Building, Symphony Hall, the Alliance Theatre Company, the Atlanta College of Art, and the Atlanta Symphony Orchestra.

Unquestionably one of the most distinctive fine arts centers in the world, Callanwolde was built in the 1920s as the home of Charles Howard Candler, eldest son of Coca-Cola founder Asa G. Candler. The magnificent estate's Irish name means "Candler's Forest." Aflame with azaleas, it is a superior setting for inspiring young artists' creative vision.

After Candler's death, the Tudor-style mansion was donated to Emory University, and has become home to several performing groups, including the Young Singers of Callanwolde, Callanwolde Theatre, Callanwolde Apprentice Dance Company, and Poetry at Callanwolde. The beautiful courtyard, with its bubbling fountain, draws children who wait while their siblings rehearse.

Each year since 1985 the Georgia Shakespeare Festival has staged a series of plays in a 110-foot circular tent on the grounds of Oglethorpe University. Prior to the performance, actors offer entertaining spoof and farce while the audience picnics on the shady grounds. After the play, guests are invited to join the director in a lively discussion about that evening's show. Some of the productions lead to symposiums. For instance, *King Lear* provided the framework for a group debate on the fragmentation of the traditional family unit, in which psychologists, clergy and family counselors all participated.

The movie and TV industries are very active in Atlanta. Over 190 productions have been filmed since 1973, such as "Home Improvement," "The Oldest Living Confederate Widow," "Robo Cop 3," "Not Without My Daughter," "Matlock," "The Big Chill," and "Smokey and the Bandit." Many of these use historic areas as backdrops, while others feature the city quite prominently. Alfred Uhry's memorable "Driving Miss Daisy" played a long engagement at Atlanta's Alliance Studio Theatre before being filmed on Lullwater Road in North Druid Hills and going on to become an Academy Award winning movie.

The Southeastern Railway Museum displays unique specimens of the railroaders' art, such as Superb, the Pullman private car used by President Warren Harding for his 1923 cross-country tour, and which later carried the casket in his funeral train. Within the Southeastern Railway Museum is the Duluth and Mt. Tabor Railway, a seven and one-half inch gauge miniature railroad. Its fully operational, coal-fired steam engines are hand-built by railroad club members. These small locomotives are surprisingly powerful, and able to pull a load of adult passengers easily.

Atlanta's climate of creative internationalism has nurtured many original artistic groups, including the Atlanta Balalaika Society Orchestra, Saint Cyril's Village Orchestra, and the Atlanta Mandolin Orchestra. Many "stars" shine in Georgia's musical firmament, such as Ray Charles, Lena Horne, James Brown, and Gladys Knight, and the city's contemporary scene continues to be lively.

# HAUTE HIGH TECH

Technology and science find the welcome mat rolled out in Georgia's capital. The city nurtures her inventive geniuses, and their successes in turn have brought the world to Atlanta's door. The Georgia Institute of Technology, for example, spends more on electrical engineering research than any other educational institution. Scientific Atlanta got its start here and

*Swan House*

*Swan House interior*

*Preserving the past*

is now the foremost manufacturer of satellite earth stations. Even the Bellsouth toll-free calling area suggests expansive development, since at 3,300 square miles it is the world's broadest.

The Fernbank Science Center boasts one of the world's largest telescopes; it was used to transmit the first live pictures of the moon as Neil Armstrong was setting foot on it in 1969. The center houses an original Apollo space capsule, an IMAX Theatre, and unique exhibits such as A Walk Through Time in Georgia. Fernbank hosted the first visit to the United States of The Great Dinosaurs of China from Inner Mongolia's Gobi Desert. This exhibit included both an eighty-five-foot long, twenty-eight-foot tall Nuoerosaurus, which is the largest assembled Cretaceous dinosaur in the world, and the hugest wooly mammoth yet unearthed.

Fernbank's Spectrum of the Senses is a hall offering intriguing experiments which children can perform themselves. Here they see tornadoes in the making, create rainbow-shaded soap bubbles four feet wide, and ponder the riddles of nature.

Behind the museum are the lush sixty-five acres of Fernbank Woods, in which nature's changing seasons can be easily observed. This virgin forest has never been logged or farmed, and provides a serene setting for peaceful walks or teaching sessions about the wonders of God's creation.

Scitrek contains no "Do Not Touch" signs. In fact, visitors are enjoined to touch everything. In one mysterious room, touching leads to photographic handprints which remain frozen on the wall for several seconds. Scitrek is considered one of the best physical science museums in America, being filled with interactive exhibits that entertain while educating.

The showpiece of the sixty-acre Atlanta Botanical Garden is the Dorothy Chapman Fuque Conservatory. In this glimmering glass cylinder are thousands of exotic species seldom seen at the same time. Arid desert is transformed to lush tropical forest, while rare birds fly free under the fifty-foot-tall canopy. Strange plants such as *welwitschia*, which has no living relatives, can be seen. Outside are Japanese, herb, rose and perennial gardens, along with the Storza Woods, one of Atlanta's few remaining natural hardwood forests. The gardens, which change through the seasons, offer an ongoing exhibit of plants which inhabit North Georgia.

Zoo Atlanta has been named one of the top ten zoos in the U.S. Visitors can view more than one thousand animals from around the world in authentic wildland environments. The zoo's Masai Mara plains, African rain forest, and Sumatran tiger forest are so naturalistic that romping elephants have been known to spray water on passers-by.

The star of the zoo is Willie B., a silverback gorilla. Named after former Atlanta mayor William B. Hartsfield, Willie B. arrived in 1961 as a two-year-old who had been captured in the wild. Living

*Robert Burns House*

*The Roosevelt's Byzantine beauty*

*The James A. Burns House, Grant Park*

*Inman Park Festival at the old Trolley Barn*

Morris Brown College

Agnes Scott College

*Emory University*

Centers for Disease Control and Prevention, Emory University

*St. Philip's Cathedral*

*The Greek Orthodox Church of the Annunciation*

*Devotion in Atlanta*

*World's First! St. John Maximovitch Eastern Orthodox Church*

*Oakland Cemetery*

*Glover Square's ornate fountain*

*Old Chamblee antique shop*

HENRY GRADY

*Davis, Lee and Jackson on Stone Mountain*

*Stone Mountain Village Craftsman*

*Rodin's L' Ombre—"The Shade"*

*Woodruff Arts Center*

Georgia Shakespeare Festival

(Opposite) Beautiful Callanwolde      Atlanta Opera performing Verdi's AIDA

*The Southeastern Railway Museum*

*St. Cyril's Village Orchestra*

*Fernbank Science Center*

*Zoo Atlanta*

*Zoo star Willie B., a Silverback Gorilla*

*Atlanta Botanical Gardens*

*CNN Center*

*Delta Airline Headquarters, Hartsfield International Airport*　　　　　*(Opposite) You'll love the way they fly!*

*The Carter Presidential Center*

*The Omni Coliseum, home of the Hawks and Knights*

*The Atlanta Knights Hockey Team*

*The Atlanta Hawks Basketball Team*

*The Georgia Dome, home of the Atlanta Falcons Football Team*

*Fulton County Stadium, home of the World Champion Atlanta Braves*

*The World Champion Atlanta Braves Baseball Team*

*Atlanta's young athletes*

*Fishing the 'Hooch*

*U.S. National Hot Air Balloon Championships*

in the zoo's rain forest, Willie B. often interrupts his schedule of food gathering and exploring to investigate visitors at close range. Atlantans are fascinated with the gorilla's fascination, and bought a TV for his cage so he could watch people more easily. Willie B. pondered the mysteries of televised football for thirty-four years as a bachelor, but finally became a father. His baby was named "Kudzu" in honor of that indefatigable Southern plant.

Atlanta's Centers for Disease Control is the country's acknowledged authority on health issues. CDC began during World War II as the Office of Malarial Control, and was expanded to become the Communicable Disease Center in 1946. With a work force of 6,500 persons, it now serves as the nation's prevention agency and has made great progress against diseases such as polio, toxic shock syndrome, swine flu, rabies, cholera, Legionnaire's disease, AIDS, and tuberculosis. Through the development of complex technological tools for combatting infectious agents, CDC played a leading role in the worldwide eradication of smallpox, and the nationwide eradication of malaria.

# A COMMUNICATIONS COMPENDIUM

Communications have been vital in Atlanta since before 1850, when over twenty different newspapers were available. Today the city supports thirty-one weeklies and seven dailies, including the *Atlanta Journal*, which "covers Dixie like the dew," and the *Atlanta Constitution,* born the same year (1868) the city got its new constitution. In 1922 the South's first radio station, WSB ("Welcome South, Brother!"), began broadcasting. The country's oldest black-owned daily also got its start here in 1928. The *Atlanta Daily World* still maintains both an office on Auburn Avenue and a significant presence in the city's journalistic community.

Always looking to the future while remembering the past, and believing that anything is possible, Atlanta's innovators have been quick to implement new communications technologies. Charles Lindbergh visited in 1927 after his historic solo flight, and sparked interest in flying. William B. Hartsfield, a great fan of aviation, recommended in 1929 that the city purchase Candler Field, formerly a two-mile auto race track, for use as an airfield. Hartsfield further lobbied for Atlanta's inclusion in the North-South Air Commerce Act mail routing. This brought in regular flights and established the city as the Southeast's aviation hub.

In 1930 Eastern Airlines made Atlanta its home base, followed by Delta Airlines in 1941. The city's rapidly expanding airport was eventually named after its greatest booster, who had in the meantime become mayor. With 1,700 daily flights, Hartsfield International is now the second busiest airport in the world in terms of passenger traffic.

In 1970 Ted Turner bought Atlanta's television channel 17, dubbed it "The Superstation," and turned what had been a losing proposition into an overnight success. In 1980 he created the world's first 24-hour news network, CNN, using the latest technology to globalize news sources.

Visitors to the stunning CNN Center are invited not only to observe "Headline News" in the making, but to participate in the process through the program "Talk Back Live." This interactive town meeting is open to a 150-member studio audience on a first-come, first-served basis. The audience may also catch a glimpse of Jane Fonda, who lives with her husband Ted in a penthouse on top of the building.

The Carter Presidential Center is dedicated to conflict resolution throughout the world, a hallmark of its founder, Jimmy Carter. Somewhat ironically, the Center is located at Copenhill, General Sherman's headquarters during the Battle of Atlanta.

The Carter Center's Library and Museum offers an intimate view of what it takes to get to the nation's highest office. Over twenty-seven million photos and mementoes document Jimmy Carter's rise from peanut farmer to governor of Georgia to the first president elected from the Deep South since the Civil War. A mock-up of the Oval Office includes a tape recording of the president's typical day at the country's rudder. Jimmy Carter himself, by means of computer technology, answers interactive questions such as "What's the best way to negotiate with terrorists?" a subject which preoccupied his time in office. Visitors can also participate in "town hall" video meetings or get information on Jimmy Carter's current programs such as Global 2000 and the Atlanta Project.

# THE SPOT FOR SPORTS

The Omni Coliseum is notable for its hot-metal "waffle iron" look. The sixteen-thousand-seat building is home to the Atlanta Hawks basketball team. In 1993-94 the Hawks distinguished themselves by winning the Central Division with the best record in the Eastern Conference. The following year, Lenny Wilkens was named the winningest coach in National Basketball Association history. The Atlanta Knights Hockey team also plays the Omni. As champions of the 1993-94 Turner Cup, the Knights like to boast, "the knightmare has come true."

*Georgia State University Apartments, part of the 1996 Olympic Village*

*(Opposite) Olympic Aquatic Center*

The Georgia Dome was the superlative setting for the 1994 Super Bowl, and it is here that the National Football League Falcons battle for supremacy. In both 1991 and 1992, the Falcons were the only NFL team with thirty or more touchdowns. In 1993, the team scored over 300 points for the fourth consecutive season.

The Dome is without contest Atlanta's most breathtaking arena. At twenty-seven stories high, it is large enough to enclose two huge C-5 transport planes. Its translucent, Teflon-coated fiberglass roof covers 8.6 acres, weighs sixty-eight tons, and is strong enough to support a loaded four-wheel-drive truck driving across it. This unique skylight illuminates the Dome interior during the day, while presenting a luminescent top to the city's evening skyline.

The Atlanta Fulton County Stadium is home for baseball's Atlanta Braves. It was here that Henry Aaron bested Babe Ruth's home run record in 1974, hitting his 715th. In 1991 a miracle occurred when the Braves went from "worst to first," winning the National League Championship. Awestruck Atlantans responded by crooning war cries and brandishing the "tomahawk chop" when the team repeated its accomplishment in 1992. Between 1991 and 1995 the Braves won their division championship (National League East) four times. In 1995 the team's persistent efforts to reach the pinnacle of baseball fame paid off: the Braves defeated the Cleveland Indians and won the World Series.

The Chattahoochee, or "Painted Rock" River, as the Cherokee Indians called it, begins just south of the Appalachian Trail near Helen, Georgia. From the mountains it weaves gently southward through Atlanta to the Apalachicola River, then on to the Gulf of Mexico. Andrew Jackson and Davy Crockett are said to have camped along its mossy banks during the Indian Wars of the 1820s. Though little more than a large creek throughout much of its Atlanta trek, the undeveloped Chattahoochee gets a lot of use from fishermen, canoers, inner tubers, and swimmers, and it supplies drinking water to cities along its route.

Booming Gwinnett County is named after Button Gwinnett, the bold Georgian who defied the colony's English-appointed governor by signing the Declaration of Independence. The county has even more than this to brag about however, such as the U.S. National Hot Air Balloon Championships, which take place at Briscoe Field. These team competitions are the first ever to be held in the United States, and draw hundreds of balloonists from all over the country. This hot air extravaganza is visible for miles, as immense witches, rabbits, dragons, shoes, and of course, spheres, float above the countryside.

As host to the 1996 Olympics, Atlanta has boosted its Sports Capital reputation to new heights.

The presence of thousands of athletes from hundreds of countries and as many cultures is a living testimonial to the city's commitment to Olympic standards.

# WHERE CIVIL RIGHTS
## CALLS HOME

The transition from segregation to integration was far less painful in Atlanta than in other cities. By 1870, Atlanta already had two blacks on its ten-man City Council. The 1890 book, *Atlanta, Gate City of the South*, records that at that time there were five colleges for blacks and only one for whites. Many individuals have been sensitive to the plight of former slaves and their descendants, but the witness of one native son captured the attention of the world.

Martin Luther King Jr. was born on Auburn Avenue in 1928. The street was then such a sizzling center of black society and entrepreneurial enterprise that it was dubbed "Sweet Auburn" by the grandfather of Maynard Jackson, Atlanta's first black mayor. Many of Atlanta's most successful African-Americans got their start on what Fortune once called the "richest Negro street in the world."

The Sweet Auburn district provided a dynamic environment for blacks, in which business, religion, art, and politics joined to create a vision of new possibilities. Just down the street from Big Bethel A.M.E. Church, the Royal Peacock Club throbbed to the music of such big name entertainers as Ray Charles (an "honorary citizen" of Atlanta), Aretha Franklin and B. B. King. Meanwhile, the nearby Atlanta Daily World, America's first black-owned daily newspaper, promised the "News While It's News!"

Martin Luther King Jr. was raised in this milieu and absorbed its mood of hopeful determination. Following in his grandfather's and father's footsteps, King pastored the Ebenezer Baptist Church, located just two blocks from his birthplace. King's preaching found its greatest resonance in articulating the sufferings of America's black community. When he spoke of the hope and dream in his heart for "freedom," he became the voice of a nationwide movement. His struggle to challenge segregation by nonviolent means won him the Nobel Peace Prize in 1965.

Guided by an abiding faith in God's providence, Dr. King founded the Southern Christian Leadership Conference and helped make Atlanta the first city in the Deep South to desegregate its schools without violence. After his 1968 assassination in Memphis, he was laid to rest in his home-

*Tomb of Dr. Martin Luther King, Jr.*

*Ebenezer Baptist Church*

*Patrick Morelli's "Behold"*

town. His tomb is lit by an eternal flame and surrounded by a five-tiered reflecting pool at the Martin Luther King Jr. Center for Nonviolent Social Change.

Across Auburn Avenue from the MLK Center stands a dramatic bronze statue crafted by Patrick Morelli. *Behold* recalls the ancient African practice of lifting a newborn baby to the sky and declaring, "Behold, the only thing greater than yourself!"

# BEYOND THE PERIMETER

Seeing all that Atlanta has to offer may take some time, yet the scenic scope is far from exhausted at the city limits! In every direction Georgia's diverse beauty will captivate and overwhelm the inquisitive visitor. An antebellum South still dripping with Spanish moss and Greek Revival mansions is not far away, and those who seek it out are sure to be entranced by what they find.

In 1828 gold was discovered in the mountains of north Georgia, producing North America's first major gold rush. Legally, the Cherokee Indians owned the land, but in 1838 Congress stripped them of their rights. Soldiers rounded up seventeen thousand Cherokees and herded them off eight hundred miles to Oklahoma. Four thousand died on that forced march, now called the "Trail of Tears."

Thousands of crazy miners swarmed into Cherokee County and the hamlet of Dahlonega (which means "precious yellow" in Cherokee) to prospect. Millions in gold were recovered, some of which was later used to sheath the state's capital building dome. It is said, though, that enough precious metal still remains in Dahlonega's hills to pave the entire square around the old court-house one foot deep!

The Dahlonega Courthouse, built in 1836, is the oldest public building in north Georgia. Its bricks and mortar, locally cast, contain traces of gold. It was from the balcony of this structure that Dahlonega mint assayer Matthew F. Stephenson attained a kind of literary immortality. Pointing to Findley Ridge before him, he uttered the words which Mark Twain immortalized in *Gilded Age* as, "There's gold in them thar hills!"

Old-time music is synonymous with the South, where the sounds of fiddles, banjos, mandolins, guitars, and dulcimers blend with intoxicating beauty. Under a shady porch, the visitor is liable to hear some great music, played just for the asking.

In spite of its pristine setting in the Blue Ridge Mountains, Helen, Georgia was for years a rather drab spot. Looking for a way to boost the town's prospects, local leaders invited an artist to restyle Helen as an "Alpine village." The main street was given a Bavarian face, and the entire town settled into charming Old-World ambience.

Helen has become the jewel of the north Georgia mountains, boasting restaurants and shops from many European cultures. Colorful wildflower festivals occur each spring, while summer brings the country rhythms of cloggers. Fall's Oktoberfest is the southeast's largest, featuring lots of beer and eight weeks of waltz and polka music by American and European German bands. The highlight of winter is Helen's *Weihnachtsmarkt,* modeled after the traditional Christmas markets of Germany.

# A GLANCE IN THE MIRROR

Cruising east on I-20 at dusk, Six Flags leads into a long hill. At its crest, a sudden breathtaking prospect appears in one's rear view mirror:

A citadel of lights rises from the murky blue of the Appalachian foothills. Around it, illuminated sentries stand at attention—a towering force of guardians seemingly frozen in gargantuan night-watch, raising defiant beacons to the edge of darkness!

But wait . . . this is no mythic scene after all, but Atlanta. The city's image so sparks the imagination that even leaving it provokes awe! Driving on, one cannot but reflect on all that this unusual community has contributed to civilization.

Atlanta is truly a town of triumph—both a dwelling-place of dreams and a rialto of reality. She has succeeded as few other places have in merging and melding opposing view-points, whether they be past and future, North and South, or black and white. It is a success born of suffering, formed in the heat of struggle—a prodigious life lesson which continues to lead the city into its own unique destiny.

Hopefully, visitors will ponder this as they commit Atlanta to fond memory. The beacons of those "guardians" which illuminate the city should suggest not merely wealth and wizardry, but wisdom. They should signify that this town, perhaps more than others, is sustained by the visions of those who believe in more than just themselves. And they should proclaim that while Atlanta is much greater than it was, it is as yet far less than it shall be.

*Bavarian Helen, Georgia*

*Mountain Musicians*

(Opposite) *The lure of the mountains*

# ABOUT THE AUTHOR

Dennis Eugene Engleman is a long-time resident of Atlanta and an electrical engineer by profession. Assisted by his wife Deborah and their three children, John Nicholas, Lily Eugenia, and Mary Victoria, he is also an active freelance writer and photographer.

Over eighty of Mr. Engleman's articles have been published in *Again, Annals of Sainte Anne de Beaupré, Axios, Catholic Twin Circle, Companion of St. Francis and St. Anthony, The Family Digest, German Life, Liguorian, Messenger of St. Anthony, Messenger of the Sacred Heart, Myrrhbearers, New Covenant, Orthodox Christian Witness, Orthodox Voices, Our Sunday Visitor, The Pilgrim, Tree of Life, The True Vine, Vista,* and other periodicals. He is also author of the book *Ultimate Things: An Orthodox Christian Perspective on the End Times* (Conciliar Press).

Mr. Engleman's photos have appeared hundreds of times in such diverse media as books, periodicals, posters, compact disc covers and refrigerator magnets. His biography is noted in various reference works, including *Who's Who in the South and Southwest.*

# ENDNOTES·


1. *Atlanta Journal/Constitution*, Sunday, July 2, 1995, p. M3.

2. Diane Coulter Thomas, *Atlanta: A City for the World* (Northridge California: Windsor Publications, 1988), 19.

3. *Oglethorpe University* 1994-1996 *Bulletin*, Oglethorpe University, p. 13.

4. *Atlanta Journal*, August 22, 1995, p. A1.

5. "The One-House Schoolroom," *Family Policy*, vol. 8, no. 4 (Sept. 1995): 6.

6. *Atlanta Journal*, August 28, 1995, p. C3.

7. *Georgia Magazine*, circa 1960, quoted in *The Historical News*, vol. 14, no. 75-GA (November 1994): 9.

*Lake Clara Meer, Piedmont Park*

*Rear Cover: The Weeping Lion of the Confederacy*